Oodles of Noodles

Contents

written by John Lockyer

Noodles are healthy food that is eaten all around the world. They are thin strips of pasta. Noodles give us energy to move, to walk, to run and to play.

Most noodles are made from wheat flour. In China and Japan, noodles are also made from rice, beans and even seaweed!

noodles

Some people make fresh noodles at home.
The flour is mixed with water to make a
dough. Sometimes eggs are mixed in, too.

4

After the dough has been rolled out very thin, it is cut into long strips with a knife or a pasta machine.

Most noodles are made in factories. Computers measure the flour and water into a large tub. In the tub, the flour and water are mixed together to make a dough.

Then the dough is put into a pressing machine, which presses it through small round holes to make noodles – oodles of noodles!
factory

Most noodles that are made in factories are dried. Noodles are dried by blasting them with hot air or by hanging them over racks.

Dried noodles can be kept for a long time before they are cooked. Fresh noodles do not keep for long. All noodles must be cooked before they are eaten.

drying racks

Noodles are quick and easy to cook, so they are a good meal for busy people. They are cooked for five to twelve minutes in boiling water.

The noodles are put onto a plate or into a bowl.
A sauce (made from tomatoes, cheese, herbs,
vegetables or meat) can be poured over them.
Noodles are also put into salads and soups.

In Italy, some noodles are called spaghetti. Spaghetti bolognese is a tasty meal. The cooked spaghetti is eaten with a delicious sauce made from tomato, beef and bacon.

In Japan, there are many noodle shops. People can choose different toppings (like fish, chicken, pork, squid, seaweed or eggs) to go with their noodles. Most people love fish soup made with thin noodles. It is very hot and spicy.

spaghetti bolognese

13

People in China eat lots of noodles. They mix them with meat, eggs, and vegetables like beans, peas and corn. Sometimes they fry the noodles to make them crispy and crunchy.

Most people use a pair of chopsticks to eat noodles, or a special spoon to eat noodle soup.

chopsticks

People have been eating noodles for thousands of years. Some people have noodles with every meal. Oodles of noodles are eaten every day!